RANJOT SINGH CHAHAL

Investing Made Easy

Finding the Right Opportunities for You

First published by Rana Books UK 2024

Copyright © 2024 by Ranjot Singh Chahal

All rights reserved. No part of this publication may be reproduced, stored or transmitted in any form or by any means, electronic, mechanical, photocopying, recording, scanning, or otherwise without written permission from the publisher. It is illegal to copy this book, post it to a website, or distribute it by any other means without permission.

First edition

Contents

Chapter 1: Understanding the Basics of Investing	1
Chapter 2: Setting Financial Goals	9
Chapter 3: Building a Diversified Investment Portfolio	15
Chapter 4: Investment Strategies and Techniques	23
Chapter 5: Understanding Market Trends and Market Analysis	29
Chapter 6: Investment Risk Management	35
Chapter 7: Investing for Retirement	41
Chapter 8: Tax Considerations in Investing	51
Chapter 9: Evaluating Investment Performance	57
Chapter 10: Investing in the Digital Age	64

Chapter 1: Understanding the Basics of Investing

In a world where financial stability and growth are paramount, understanding the basics of investing is crucial. Investing is not just about putting money into various assets; it is about making informed decisions that can generate income or increase wealth over time. This chapter will delve into the fundamental concepts of investing, the benefits it provides, and the different types of investments available to investors.

Section 1: What is Investing?

Investing is the act of committing money or capital to an asset or endeavor with the expectation of generating returns or profit in the future. It involves allocating resources in a way that is expected to generate income or appreciate in value over time. Unlike saving, which typically involves depositing money in a bank account or similar low-risk instruments, investing usually carries some level of risk in pursuit of higher returns.

Investing can take various forms, from buying stocks and bonds to investing in real estate, starting a business, or even investing in collectibles like art or vintage cars. The goal of investing is to grow wealth or preserve capital over the long term through strategic decision-making and risk management.

Examples of investing include:

1. Stock Market Investing: Buying shares of publicly traded companies with the expectation that their value will increase over time, allowing investors to benefit from capital appreciation and dividends.

2. Real Estate Investing: Purchasing properties such as residential homes, commercial buildings, or rental units with the goal of generating rental income and capital gains through property appreciation.

3. Mutual Funds: Investing in a pool of funds managed by professionals who allocate investments across various assets like stocks, bonds, and other securities to diversify risk and optimize returns.

4. Retirement Accounts: Contributing to retirement accounts like 401(k) or Individual Retirement Accounts (IRAs) to grow savings over time through investments in stocks, bonds, and other financial instruments tailored to retirement goals.

5. Peer-to-Peer Lending: Investing in peer-to-peer lending platforms where investors can lend money to individuals or small businesses in exchange for interest payments on the loans.

Overall, investing plays a vital role in building wealth, achieving financial goals, and securing a stable financial future. By understanding the principles of investing and making informed decisions, individuals can harness the power of compounding returns to grow their assets over time.

Section 2: Benefits of Investing

Investing offers a multitude of benefits that go beyond simply preserving capital. Whether you are looking to grow your wealth, generate passive income, or achieve long-term financial goals, investing can be a powerful tool for achieving financial success. Some key benefits of investing include:

1. Wealth Accumulation: Investing provides the opportunity to grow wealth over time through the power of compounding returns. By reinvesting earnings and allowing investments to grow, individuals can significantly increase their net worth over the long term.

2. Passive Income: Many investment vehicles, such as rental properties, dividend-paying stocks, and bonds, generate regular income streams that can provide a source of passive income. This can help diversify income sources and create financial stability.

3. Portfolio Diversification: Investing in a variety of assets, such as stocks, bonds, real estate, and alternative investments, helps spread risk and reduce exposure to any single asset class. Diversification can help protect a portfolio from market volatility and optimize risk-adjusted returns.

4. Hedge Against Inflation: Investing in assets that have the potential to grow in value over time can provide a hedge against inflation. As the purchasing power of money declines due to rising prices, investments that outpace inflation can help preserve wealth.

5. Financial Goals Achievement: Whether it's saving for retirement, buying a home, funding education, or starting a business, investing can help individuals achieve their financial goals by generating returns that align with their objectives.

6. Tax Efficiency: Certain investment vehicles offer tax advantages, such as retirement accounts, tax-advantaged savings plans, and capital gains tax treatment. By investing strategically and leveraging tax-efficient strategies, investors can minimize tax liabilities and maximize after-tax returns.

7. Wealth Preservation: Investing in assets that appreciate in value can help preserve and protect wealth for future generations. By growing assets over time, individuals can build a legacy and secure financial stability for themselves and their families.

Overall, the benefits of investing extend beyond financial returns; it encompasses wealth creation, income generation, risk management, and goal achievement. By understanding the advantages of investing and incorporating it into a comprehensive financial plan, individuals can pave the way for a prosperous and secure financial future.

Section 3: Types of Investments

CHAPTER 1: UNDERSTANDING THE BASICS OF INVESTING

Investors have a wide range of investment options available to suit their risk tolerance, financial goals, and investment preferences. Understanding the different types of investments can help individuals tailor their investment portfolios to achieve their objectives effectively. Some common types of investments include:

1. Stocks: Stocks represent ownership in a company and provide investors with a share of the company's profits through dividends and capital appreciation. Investing in stocks carries varying levels of risk depending on the company's performance, industry trends, and market conditions.

Example: An investor buys shares of a technology company with strong growth prospects, aiming to benefit from capital appreciation as the company expands its market share and revenue streams.

2. Bonds: Bonds are debt securities issued by governments, municipalities, or corporations to raise capital. Investors who buy bonds are essentially lending money to the issuer in exchange for periodic interest payments and the return of the principal at maturity.

Example: An investor purchases government bonds to generate steady income through interest payments while preserving capital in a relatively low-risk investment.

3. Real Estate: Real estate investments involve purchasing properties such as residential homes, rental units, commercial buildings, or land with the goal of generating rental income,

capital appreciation, or both.

Example: A real estate investor buys rental properties in a high-demand market, leasing them to tenants and earning rental income while benefiting from property appreciation over time.

4. Mutual Funds: Mutual funds pool money from multiple investors to invest in a diversified portfolio of stocks, bonds, or other securities managed by professional portfolio managers. Investors can access diversified investment strategies and benefit from professional management.

Example: An investor chooses to invest in a mutual fund that tracks the performance of the S&P 500 index, providing exposure to a broad range of large-cap U.S. companies and diversifying market risk.

5. Exchange-Traded Funds (ETFs): ETFs are similar to mutual funds but trade on stock exchanges like individual stocks. ETFs offer diversification, liquidity, and low expense ratios, making them popular investment vehicles for many investors.

Example: An investor buys shares of an ETF that tracks a specific sector index, such as healthcare or technology, to gain exposure to industry-specific stocks and capitalize on sector trends.

6. Commodities: Commodities include physical goods such as gold, silver, oil, agricultural products, and industrial metals. Investors can invest in commodities directly through futures contracts, commodity-linked ETFs, or commodity-focused mutual funds to diversify their portfolios and hedge against

inflation.

Example: An investor allocates a portion of their portfolio to gold by purchasing gold bullion or investing in a gold ETF as a hedge against economic uncertainty and currency devaluation.

7. Alternative Investments: Alternative investments encompass a broad range of assets beyond traditional stocks and bonds, such as private equity, hedge funds, real assets, collectibles, and cryptocurrencies. These investments offer unique risk-return profiles and diversification benefits.

Example: An investor diversifies their portfolio by allocating capital to a private equity fund that invests in early-stage startups, aiming to benefit from potential high-growth opportunities and private market returns.

By understanding the characteristics, risk profiles, and potential returns of different types of investments, investors can construct well-balanced portfolios that align with their financial goals, time horizons, and risk preferences. Diversification across asset classes and investment strategies can help optimize returns, minimize risk, and achieve long-term financial success.

Conclusion

In conclusion, understanding the basics of investing is essential for individuals seeking to build wealth, achieve financial goals, and secure a stable financial future. By grasping the concept of investing, exploring the benefits it offers, and familiarizing themselves with the various types of investments available, investors can make informed decisions and create portfolios that align with their objectives.

Investing is not just about choosing assets and hoping for the best; it involves strategic planning, risk management, and continuous learning to navigate the complexities of financial markets successfully. Whether you are a novice investor looking to start your investment journey or an experienced investor seeking to enhance your portfolio, mastering the fundamentals of investing is key to building a solid financial foundation and pursuing long-term prosperity.

By recognizing the power of compounding returns, the importance of diversification, and the role of risk management in investing, individuals can harness the potential of financial markets to grow wealth, generate income, and achieve financial independence. Through education, research, and prudent decision-making, investors can unlock the doors to a world of opportunities and set themselves on a path to financial success.

In the next chapter, we will delve deeper into the principles of risk management, portfolio construction, and investment strategies to further enhance your understanding of investing and empower you to make informed decisions in pursuit of your financial goals. Stay tuned for an in-depth exploration of advanced investing concepts and practical strategies to help you navigate the complexities of financial markets with confidence and clarity.

Chapter 2: Setting Financial Goals

In this chapter, we will delve into the critical aspects of setting financial goals, which play a crucial role in shaping your investment journey. Setting clear and achievable financial goals is a fundamental step towards building a robust investment strategy that aligns with your aspirations and risk tolerance. To effectively navigate the complex world of investments, one must begin by identifying investment objectives, determining risk tolerance, and setting realistic investment goals.

Identifying Your Investment Objectives

The first step in setting financial goals is identifying your investment objectives. These objectives serve as the guiding principles that shape your investment decisions and help in determining the most suitable investment strategies to achieve them. Identifying investment objectives involves defining what you aim to achieve through your investments and understanding your financial needs, aspirations, and time horizon.

There are several common investment objectives that individuals may have:

1. Wealth Preservation: Some investors prioritize capital preservation and focus on safeguarding their wealth rather than aggressively seeking high returns. This objective is often suited for more conservative investors who prioritize minimizing risk.

2. Capital Growth: Investors seeking capital growth aim to increase the value of their investments over time. They are willing to take on a higher level of risk in pursuit of potentially higher returns.

3. Income Generation: Investors looking for regular income streams prioritize investments that generate consistent income, such as dividend-paying stocks, bonds, or real estate properties.

4. Retirement Planning: Many individuals invest with the goal of building a retirement fund that will sustain them during their retirement years. They may focus on long-term growth and income generation to secure their financial future.

5. Education Funding: Parents may invest with the objective of building a fund to finance their children's education expenses. This goal requires a specific time horizon and investment strategy aligned with the expected educational expenses.

6. Wealth Accumulation: Investors aiming to accumulate significant wealth over time set their sights on growing their assets through strategic investment decisions.

It is essential to prioritize and rank your investment objectives based on your financial circumstances and future goals. Understanding your investment objectives will help you tailor your investment portfolio to meet your specific needs and objectives. For example, if your primary objective is retirement planning, you may opt for long-term growth-oriented investments like equities, whereas if your goal is to generate regular income, you may focus on fixed-income investments like bonds.

Determining Your Risk Tolerance

Risk tolerance refers to your ability and willingness to endure fluctuations in the value of your investments. Understanding your risk tolerance is crucial in determining the appropriate asset allocation and investment strategy that aligns with your comfort level and financial goals. Every individual has a unique risk tolerance based on various factors such as age, financial situation, investment knowledge, and psychological makeup.

There are generally three main categories of risk tolerance:

1. Conservative: Conservative investors have a low tolerance for risk and prefer investments with lower volatility and a higher degree of capital preservation. They are more averse to fluctuations in the value of their investments and prioritize stability over potential high returns.

2. Moderate: Moderate investors are willing to accept a moderate level of risk in exchange for potentially higher returns. They seek a balance between generating growth and preserving capital and are comfortable with a mix of riskier and more stable investment options.

3. Aggressive: Aggressive investors have a high tolerance for

risk and are willing to accept significant fluctuations in the value of their investments in pursuit of higher returns. They prioritize capital growth over stability and are more inclined towards high-risk, high-reward investments such as equities or speculative assets.

To determine your risk tolerance, you can use various risk assessment tools provided by financial institutions or work with a financial advisor who can help gauge your comfort level with risk. Factors such as your investment time horizon, financial goals, income stability, and psychological mindset play a crucial role in determining your risk tolerance.

Assessing your risk tolerance involves considering how you would react to market fluctuations, economic uncertainties, and potential losses in your investment portfolio. It is important to strike a balance between your risk tolerance and investment objectives to build a well-structured and resilient investment portfolio that can weather market volatility.

Setting Realistic Investment Goals

Setting realistic investment goals is essential for creating a clear roadmap that outlines your financial objectives and the steps required to achieve them. Realistic investment goals are specific, measurable, achievable, relevant, and time-bound (SMART), helping you stay focused and disciplined in pursuing your financial ambitions.

Here are some key principles to consider when setting realistic investment goals:

1. Specific: Your investment goals should be specific and well-defined. Rather than setting broad objectives like "make money," articulate precise goals such as "achieve a 10% annual return on my investment portfolio" or "save $500 per month for retirement."

2. Measurable: Your investment goals should be quantifiable so that you can track your progress. Establish milestones and benchmarks to gauge your performance and make adjustments as needed to stay on track.

3. Achievable: Your investment goals should be realistic and attainable based on your financial capacity, risk tolerance, and time horizon. Setting unattainable goals can lead to frustration and disappointment, while achievable goals provide a sense of accomplishment and motivation.

4. Relevant: Make sure your investment goals are aligned with your overall financial objectives and aspirations. Your investment goals should support your long-term financial well-being and cater to your specific needs and priorities.

5. Time-Bound: Set clear timeframes for achieving your investment goals to create a sense of urgency and accountability. Divide your goals into short-term, medium-term, and long-term targets with specific deadlines to monitor progress effectively.

Examples of realistic investment goals based on the SMART criteria include:

- Short-Term Goal: Save $2,000 in an emergency fund within the next six months to cover unexpected expenses without dipping into savings or incurring debt.

- Medium-Term Goal: Generate a passive income stream of $500 per month from dividend-paying stocks within two years to supplement regular income.

- Long-Term Goal: Build a retirement portfolio with a target of $1 million in savings by age 60 by contributing a set amount each month and adjusting investments based on performance.

By setting realistic investment goals that are well-defined and aligned with your financial objectives, you can create a solid foundation for your investment strategy and monitor your progress effectively.

In conclusion, setting financial goals is a crucial step in the investment process that lays the groundwork for a successful investment journey. By identifying your investment objectives, determining your risk tolerance, and setting realistic investment goals, you can establish a clear roadmap that guides your investment decisions and helps you achieve your financial aspirations. Remember to review and adjust your financial goals periodically to adapt to changing circumstances and ensure that your investment strategy remains relevant and effective.

By incorporating the insights and principles outlined in this chapter, you can build a robust investment framework tailored to your unique needs and objectives. Stay focused, disciplined, and informed throughout your investment journey to maximize your chances of achieving long-term financial success.

Chapter 3: Building a Diversified Investment Portfolio

In the realm of personal finance and wealth management, one aspect that often takes center stage is the construction of a well-diversified investment portfolio. This entails spreading your investments across different asset classes, such as stocks, bonds, real estate, and others, to mitigate risks and maximize returns. Chapter 3 delves into the importance of diversification, various asset allocation strategies, and the merits of investing in stocks, bonds, and real estate.

Importance of Diversification:

Diversification is a fundamental principle in investing that aims to reduce risk by spreading investments across different asset classes and instruments. The rationale behind diversification is rooted in the concept of not putting all your eggs in one basket. By diversifying, investors can potentially minimize the impact of adverse events on their overall portfolio performance.

1. Risk Mitigation: The primary motivation behind diversification is risk mitigation. Different asset classes behave differently

under various market conditions. For instance, stocks are often considered riskier but offer higher potential returns, while bonds provide more stability but with lower returns. By holding a mix of assets, an investor can reduce the impact of a downturn in any single asset class.

2. Volatility Smoothing: Diversification can help smooth out the volatility of a portfolio. When one asset class experiences a sharp decline, other asset classes may provide stability or even positive returns, thus buffering the overall impact on the portfolio.

3. Enhanced Returns: While the primary aim of diversification is risk reduction, it can also potentially enhance returns. By investing in assets with non-correlated or negatively correlated returns, the performance of one asset can offset the performance of another, leading to improved risk-adjusted returns.

4. Liquidity Management: Diversification can also aid in managing liquidity needs. By allocating investments across different asset classes with varying liquidity profiles, investors can ensure they have access to funds when needed without having to liquidate all their holdings at unfavorable times.

5. Psychological Benefits: Diversification can provide psychological benefits by reducing the anxiety associated with monitoring the performance of a concentrated portfolio. Knowing that your investments are spread across various avenues can offer peace of mind during turbulent market conditions.

Asset Allocation Strategies:

CHAPTER 3: BUILDING A DIVERSIFIED INVESTMENT PORTFOLIO

Asset allocation is the process of dividing investments among different asset classes based on factors such as risk tolerance, investment horizon, and financial goals. Various strategies exist to determine the optimal mix of assets in a portfolio. Some common asset allocation strategies include:

1. Strategic Asset Allocation: Strategic asset allocation involves setting a target allocation for different asset classes based on long-term investment objectives and risk tolerance. This strategy aims to maintain a consistent allocation over time through periodic rebalancing.

Example: An investor with a long-term horizon and moderate risk tolerance might opt for a strategic asset allocation of 60% stocks, 30% bonds, and 10% real estate.

2. Tactical Asset Allocation: Tactical asset allocation involves making short-term adjustments to the portfolio based on economic conditions, market trends, or valuation metrics. This strategy allows for deviations from the strategic allocation to capitalize on perceived opportunities or mitigate risks.

Example: During periods of economic uncertainty, an investor may increase the allocation to defensive sectors like utilities and consumer staples while reducing exposure to cyclical sectors like technology and industrials.

3. Dynamic Asset Allocation: Dynamic asset allocation combines elements of both strategic and tactical approaches by allowing for adjustments to the long-term allocation based on prevailing market conditions. This strategy seeks to capitalize on short-

term opportunities while maintaining a core strategic framework.

Example: A dynamic asset allocation strategy may involve overweighting equities during periods of economic expansion and shifting towards bonds or cash during bear markets.

4. Risk Parity: Risk parity is an asset allocation strategy that seeks to allocate investments based on the risk contribution of each asset class rather than the traditional market value weighting. This approach aims to balance the risk exposure across asset classes, allowing for more consistent risk-adjusted returns.

Example: In a risk parity portfolio, assets with lower volatility, such as bonds, may receive a higher allocation to achieve a more balanced risk profile compared to assets with higher volatility, like stocks.

Investing in Stocks, Bonds, and Real Estate:

Stocks, bonds, and real estate are among the most common asset classes in an investment portfolio, each offering unique characteristics and serving different objectives. Understanding the merits of investing in each asset class is crucial for building a well-diversified portfolio.

1. Investing in Stocks:

Stocks, or equities, represent ownership in a company and provide investors with the potential for capital appreciation and dividends. Investing in stocks offers the following benefits:

- Growth Potential: Historically, stocks have provided higher returns compared to other asset classes over the long term. By investing in well-managed companies with strong growth prospects, investors can benefit from capital appreciation as the value of their shares increases.

- Diversification: Stocks represent ownership in companies across different sectors and industries, allowing investors to achieve diversification within the equity portion of their portfolio. By investing in a mix of large-cap, mid-cap, and small-cap stocks, investors can spread their risk within the equity market.

- Dividend Income: Many companies pay dividends to their shareholders as a share of their profits. Dividend-paying stocks can provide a steady income stream, making them attractive for investors seeking regular cash flow along with the potential for stock price appreciation.

Example: An investor looking for long-term growth might consider investing in technology stocks like Apple or Microsoft, which have demonstrated consistent growth and innovation in their respective industries.

2. Investing in Bonds:

Bonds are debt securities issued by governments, municipalities, or corporations to raise capital. Investing in bonds offers the following benefits:

- Income Generation: Bonds pay regular interest payments to investors, providing a predictable income stream. Fixed-income securities like bonds are often considered more stable than stocks and can serve as a source of passive income for investors.

- Capital Preservation: Bonds are generally less volatile than stocks and are considered a safer investment option for preserving capital. Government bonds, in particular, are often perceived as low-risk investments due to the creditworthiness of the issuing entity.

- Diversification: Bonds exhibit different risk-return characteristics compared to stocks, making them an essential component of a diversified portfolio. By holding a mix of government, corporate, and municipal bonds, investors can reduce the overall risk of their portfolio.

Example: An investor nearing retirement might consider allocating a significant portion of their portfolio to high-quality bonds, such as U.S. Treasury bonds or investment-grade corporate bonds, to provide income and preserve capital.

3. Investing in Real Estate:

Real estate investments involve owning physical properties or investing in real estate investment trusts (REITs) that own and operate income-generating properties. Investing in real estate offers the following benefits:

- Income Potential: Real estate investments can generate rental income from residential, commercial, or industrial properties. Rental yields can provide a steady cash flow stream for investors seeking regular income in addition to potential capital appreciation.

- Diversification: Real estate has a low correlation with traditional financial assets like stocks and bonds, making it an effective diversifier in a portfolio. Real estate tends to follow its own market cycles, which can help reduce overall portfolio volatility.

- Hedge Against Inflation: Real estate is often considered a tangible asset that can hedge against inflation. Property values and rental income tend to increase in line with inflation, providing investors with a natural inflation hedge.

Example: An investor interested in real estate but seeking liquidity and diversification might consider investing in publicly traded REITs, which offer exposure to a diversified portfolio of properties without the need for direct property ownership.

Conclusion:

Building a diversified investment portfolio is a crucial step in achieving long-term financial goals while managing risks effectively. Diversification allows investors to spread their investments across different asset classes, reducing concentration risk and enhancing portfolio resilience. By employing various asset allocation strategies and investing in stocks, bonds, and real estate, investors can create a well-rounded portfolio that balances risk and return objectives.

It is essential for investors to assess their risk tolerance, investment horizon, and financial goals before constructing a diversified portfolio. Regular monitoring and periodic rebalancing are necessary to ensure that the portfolio remains aligned with the investor's objectives and risk profile. By understanding the importance of diversification, implementing sound asset allocation strategies, and leveraging the benefits of different asset classes, investors can build a robust investment portfolio that stands the test of time.

Chapter 4: Investment Strategies and Techniques

In the world of investing, there are a multitude of strategies and techniques that investors can employ to achieve their financial goals. Whether you are a seasoned investor or just starting out, understanding different investment strategies is crucial for making informed decisions about where to put your money. In this chapter, we will delve deep into some key investment strategies and techniques, including long-term vs. short-term investing, value investing, growth investing, dividend investing, and dollar-cost averaging.

1. Long-Term vs. Short-Term Investing

One of the fundamental decisions that investors face is whether to focus on long-term or short-term investing. Long-term investing involves holding onto investments for an extended period, often years or even decades. The goal of long-term investing is to capitalize on the power of compounding returns and benefit from the overall growth of the market over time. Long-term investors tend to have a more patient and passive approach to investing, relying on the principle that quality investments will appreciate in value over the long run.

On the other hand, short-term investing involves buying and selling securities within a relatively short time frame, often days, weeks, or months. Short-term investors aim to profit from short-term price fluctuations in the market. Short-term trading strategies can be more active and speculative compared to long-term investing, as they rely on timing the market and taking advantage of short-lived opportunities.

Example: Long-Term vs. Short-Term Investing

Suppose you have $10,000 to invest in the stock market. You can choose to invest in a diversified portfolio of blue-chip stocks and hold onto them for the next 10 years, expecting steady growth in line with historical market returns. This would be an example of long-term investing.

Alternatively, you could decide to try your hand at day trading, buying and selling stocks based on short-term price movements. You might buy a stock in the morning and sell it by the end of the day if you believe it will see a quick price increase. This would be an example of short-term investing.

2. Value Investing

Value investing is an investment strategy popularized by legendary investor Benjamin Graham and later refined by his student Warren Buffett. The basic principle of value investing is to identify undervalued securities trading at a price below their intrinsic value. Value investors believe that markets can be inefficient and that there are opportunities to buy quality assets at a discount.

Value investors typically look for stocks with strong fundamentals, such as low price-to-earnings ratios, solid balance sheets, and consistent earnings growth. They seek to invest in companies that are trading at a discount to their intrinsic value, with the expectation that the market will eventually recognize the true worth of the stock and drive its price higher.

Example: Value Investing

Let's say you analyze a company that has a strong brand, solid financials, but its stock price has recently fallen due to a temporary market downturn. As a value investor, you see this as an opportunity to buy the stock at a discount compared to its real worth. You decide to invest in the company with the expectation that its stock price will eventually rise to reflect its true value.

3. Growth Investing

Growth investing is another popular investment strategy that focuses on investing in companies with high growth potential. Growth investors look for companies that are expected to grow earnings and revenue at an above-average rate compared to the overall market. These companies often operate in fast-growing industries and reinvest their profits back into the business to fuel future growth.

Growth investors are willing to pay a premium for these high-growth companies, as they believe that the potential future returns will justify the higher valuation. They are looking for companies that have a competitive advantage, a strong track record of growth, and a clear path to continued expansion.

Example: Growth Investing

Imagine you come across a technology startup that is developing cutting-edge artificial intelligence technology with the potential to revolutionize the industry. The company has shown impressive revenue growth in recent years and has a clear strategy for expanding its market reach. As a growth investor, you see the opportunity for substantial returns if the company can continue its growth trajectory and capitalize on its innovative technology.

4. Dividend Investing

Dividend investing is a strategy that focuses on investing in companies that pay regular dividends to their shareholders. Dividends are payments made by companies to distribute a portion of their profits to shareholders. Dividend investors seek out companies that have a history of paying consistent dividends and have the potential to increase payouts over time.

Dividend investing is popular among income-oriented investors who are looking for a regular stream of passive income from their investments. Dividend-paying stocks are often seen as more stable and less volatile than growth stocks, as they provide a steady income stream regardless of market fluctuations.

Example: Dividend Investing

Suppose you are nearing retirement and looking to build a

portfolio that generates a reliable income stream. You decide to invest in a diversified portfolio of blue-chip stocks that have a track record of paying consistent dividends. These companies are well-established, profitable, and have a history of increasing their dividend payments over time. By focusing on dividend-paying stocks, you aim to create a source of passive income to support your retirement lifestyle.

5. Dollar-Cost Averaging

Dollar-cost averaging is an investment strategy that involves investing a fixed amount of money at regular intervals, regardless of market conditions. With dollar-cost averaging, investors buy more shares when prices are low and fewer shares when prices are high. This approach helps to mitigate the impact of market volatility and can result in a lower average cost per share over time.

Dollar-cost averaging is a disciplined and systematic approach to investing that removes the need to time the market. By investing consistently over time, investors can take advantage of market fluctuations to build a diversified portfolio at an affordable average price.

Example: Dollar-Cost Averaging

Suppose you decide to invest $500 in a particular stock every month through a dollar-cost averaging strategy. In the first month, the stock price is $50 per share, so you buy 10 shares. In the second month, the price drops to $40 per share, allowing you to purchase 12.5 shares with your $500. Over the following months, the stock price fluctuates, but you continue to invest

$500 each month. By the end of the year, you have accumulated a significant number of shares at an average cost that reflects a blend of high and low prices.

In conclusion, understanding different investment strategies and techniques is essential for investors looking to build a successful investment portfolio. Whether you prefer long-term or short-term investing, value investing, growth investing, dividend investing, or dollar-cost averaging, each strategy has its own set of benefits and risks. By carefully considering your financial goals, risk tolerance, and investment horizon, you can choose the strategies that align best with your objectives and set yourself up for long-term success in the world of investing.

Chapter 5: Understanding Market Trends and Market Analysis

Market trends and analysis play a crucial role in helping investors and traders make informed decisions in the financial markets. By understanding market trends and conducting market analysis, individuals can identify potential opportunities, minimize risks, and optimize their investment strategies. This chapter will delve into various aspects of market trends and analysis, including fundamental analysis, technical analysis, market timing, and market cycles.

1. Fundamental Analysis

Fundamental analysis is a method of evaluating securities by analyzing various factors that could affect their value. This form of analysis involves examining the financial health and performance of a company, its industry, and the broader economy to determine the intrinsic value of a security. Fundamental analysis helps investors identify undervalued or overvalued assets based on their underlying economic factors.

Key components of fundamental analysis include:

a. Financial Statements: Investors analyze a company's financial statements, including the income statement, balance sheet, and cash flow statement, to assess its financial health and performance.

b. Economic Indicators: Analysts consider various economic indicators, such as GDP growth, inflation rates, interest rates, and employment data, to understand the broader economic environment in which a company operates.

c. Industry Analysis: Assessing the competitive landscape, market dynamics, and growth prospects of a specific industry helps investors gauge the future potential of companies operating within that sector.

d. Company Valuation: Fundamental analysis uses valuation metrics like price-to-earnings (P/E) ratio, price-to-book (P/B) ratio, and dividend yield to determine whether a stock is undervalued or overvalued relative to its intrinsic value.

Example: Suppose an investor conducts fundamental analysis on a technology company by examining its financial statements, competitive positioning in the industry, growth prospects, and valuation metrics. Based on this analysis, the investor concludes that the stock is undervalued compared to its peers and decides to buy shares in the company.

2. Technical Analysis

Technical analysis is the study of past market data, primarily price and volume, to forecast future price movements. Unlike fundamental analysis, which focuses on intrinsic value, technical analysis relies on historical price patterns and market trends to identify potential trading opportunities. Technical analysts use charts, indicators, and statistical tools to interpret market behavior and make trading decisions.

Key components of technical analysis include:

a. Price Charts: Technical analysts use price charts, such as line charts, bar charts, and candlestick charts, to visualize historical price movements and identify patterns that could indicate future price directions.

b. Technical Indicators: Indicators like moving averages, relative strength index (RSI), and moving average convergence divergence (MACD) help traders analyze market trends, momentum, and potential reversal points.

c. Support and Resistance Levels: Traders look for key support and resistance levels on price charts to identify potential buying or selling opportunities based on how the price reacts at these levels.

d. Trend Analysis: Technical analysts use trend lines and trend channels to identify the prevailing market trends, such as uptrends, downtrends, or sideways trends, and make informed trading decisions.

Example: A technical analyst studies a stock chart and notices a bullish pattern known as a "cup and handle" formation, indicating a potential uptrend. Using technical indicators like the moving average crossover and RSI, the analyst confirms the bullish signal and decides to buy the stock.

3. Market Timing

Market timing refers to the strategy of buying and selling financial assets based on predictions of future market movements. Investors who engage in market timing attempt to enter and exit positions at opportune times to capitalize on expected price trends. While successful market timing can lead to substantial profits, it can also be challenging and involves significant risks, including the potential for missed opportunities and losses.

Key considerations for market timing include:

a. Economic Data: Market timers monitor economic data releases, central bank policies, and geopolitical events to anticipate how these factors could impact market movements and adjust their positions accordingly.

b. Technical Signals: Market timers use technical analysis tools and indicators to identify potential entry and exit points based on price patterns, momentum, and trend reversals in the market.

c. Sentiment Analysis: Monitoring market sentiment, investor behavior, and media coverage can provide insights into market psychology and help market timers assess the prevailing market sentiment.

d. Risk Management: Effective risk management is essential for market timing strategies to mitigate potential losses and preserve capital in case of adverse market movements.

Example: A market timer predicts that a stock market correction is imminent based on overbought conditions and divergences in technical indicators. To avoid potential losses, the market timer decides to sell a portion of their equity holdings and increase their cash position until the correction unfolds.

4. Market Cycles

Market cycles refer to the recurring patterns of alternating between expansion and contraction phases in financial markets. Understanding market cycles can help investors anticipate changing market conditions, identify potential turning points, and adjust their investment strategies accordingly. Market cycles are influenced by various factors, including economic trends, investor sentiment, and policy changes.

Key phases of market cycles include:

a. Expansion: During the expansion phase, economic growth accelerates, businesses thrive, and asset prices generally rise. Investor confidence is high, leading to bullish market sentiment and increased risk appetite.

b. Peak: The peak represents the highest point of the market cycle when asset prices reach their peak levels, valuations become stretched, and speculative behavior increases. Signs of excess leverage and euphoria may signal an impending market downturn.

c. Contraction: In the contraction phase, economic growth slows down, corporate earnings decline, and asset prices start to fall. Investor sentiment turns bearish as uncertainty and risk aversion rise, leading to market corrections or downturns.

d. Trough: The trough marks the lowest point of the market cycle when asset prices bottom out, investor pessimism reaches a peak, and opportunities for value investing emerge. The trough phase sets the stage for the next expansionary cycle.

Example: An investor recognizes that the stock market is in the late stages of the expansion phase, characterized by high valuations, low volatility, and excessive risk-taking behavior. Anticipating a potential market correction, the investor reallocates their portfolio to defensive assets and reduces exposure to high-risk equities.

In conclusion, understanding market trends and conducting thorough market analysis are essential for making informed investment decisions and navigating the dynamic landscape of financial markets. By incorporating fundamental analysis, technical analysis, market timing, and an awareness of market cycles into their investment strategies, individuals can enhance their chances of achieving their financial goals and managing risk effectively. Continuous monitoring of market trends and staying informed about economic developments are key to adapting to changing market conditions and optimizing investment outcomes.

Chapter 6: Investment Risk Management

Investment risk management is a crucial aspect of financial planning that aims to both assess and mitigate risks that investors face in the pursuit of financial returns. In this chapter, we will delve deeply into three key components of investment risk management: risk assessment, risk mitigation strategies, and the importance of emergency funds.

Risk Assessment:

Risk assessment is the process of identifying, analyzing, and evaluating potential risks associated with an investment. It is essential for investors to have a clear understanding of the risks they face to make informed decisions and develop effective risk management strategies. There are various types of risks that investors may encounter, including market risk, credit risk, liquidity risk, inflation risk, interest rate risk, and more.

1. Market Risk: Market risk is the risk of losses resulting from changes in market prices, such as stock prices, bond prices, or exchange rates. For example, if an investor holds a portfolio of

stocks and the stock market experiences a downturn, the value of the portfolio may decline.

2. Credit Risk: Credit risk refers to the risk of default by a borrower or issuer of a financial instrument. Investors face credit risk when investing in bonds, loans, or other fixed-income securities. For instance, if a company defaults on its bonds, bondholders may incur losses.

3. Liquidity Risk: Liquidity risk is the risk of not being able to sell an investment quickly without significantly impacting its price. Illiquid investments can be difficult to sell, especially during periods of market stress. Real estate and certain types of alternative investments are examples of investments that may pose liquidity risk.

4. Inflation Risk: Inflation risk, also known as purchasing power risk, is the risk that the returns on an investment may not keep pace with inflation, leading to a decrease in real purchasing power. Investors often seek inflation-protected securities or assets like real estate and commodities to hedge against inflation risk.

5. Interest Rate Risk: Interest rate risk is the risk of losses resulting from changes in interest rates. For example, if an investor holds fixed-rate bonds and interest rates rise, the value of the bonds in the secondary market may decrease. Conversely, falling interest rates can increase the value of existing bonds.

Risk Mitigation Strategies:

CHAPTER 6: INVESTMENT RISK MANAGEMENT

Once investors have identified the potential risks they face, they can implement various risk mitigation strategies to manage and reduce these risks. Effective risk mitigation strategies aim to protect investments against adverse events and limit downside risk. Some common risk mitigation strategies include diversification, asset allocation, hedging, and using derivatives.

1. Diversification: Diversification is a risk management strategy that involves spreading investments across different asset classes, sectors, industries, and geographic regions. By diversifying their portfolios, investors can reduce the impact of individual investment losses on their overall wealth. For example, an investor may hold a mix of stocks, bonds, real estate, and commodities to achieve diversification.

2. Asset Allocation: Asset allocation is the strategic distribution of investments across different asset classes based on an investor's risk tolerance, time horizon, and financial goals. By diversifying investment holdings among asset classes such as stocks, bonds, and cash equivalents, investors can achieve a balanced portfolio that aligns with their risk appetite and return objectives.

3. Hedging: Hedging is a risk management strategy that involves using financial instruments or strategies to offset the risk of adverse price movements in the market. For example, investors can hedge against market risk by using options contracts to protect their portfolios from downside movements in stock prices. Similarly, currency hedging can help investors mitigate the impact of exchange rate fluctuations on foreign investments.

4. Derivatives: Derivatives are financial instruments whose value is derived from an underlying asset, index, or security. Investors can use derivatives such as options, futures, and swaps to hedge against specific risks or to speculate on future price movements. For instance, an investor may use put options to protect their portfolio against downside risk or use futures contracts to hedge against commodity price fluctuations.

Importance of Emergency Funds:

In addition to assessing and mitigating investment risks, investors should also prioritize building emergency funds to safeguard against unforeseen financial emergencies and unexpected expenses. An emergency fund is a reserve of liquid assets set aside to cover living expenses and essential bills in the event of job loss, medical emergencies, or other financial crises.

1. Financial Stability: An emergency fund provides a financial safety net that can help individuals and families weather unexpected setbacks without relying on high-interest debt or liquidating investments. By having an emergency fund, investors can maintain financial stability and avoid financial distress during challenging times.

2. Peace of Mind: Knowing that they have a buffer of savings to fall back on can give investors peace of mind and reduce anxiety about financial uncertainty. An emergency fund can provide a sense of security and confidence that they can handle unexpected expenses without compromising their long-term financial goals.

3. Avoiding Debt: In the absence of an emergency fund, individuals may be forced to resort to borrowing money through credit cards, personal loans, or other forms of debt to cover emergency expenses. Accumulating high-interest debt can lead to financial stress and hinder wealth-building efforts over time. Having an emergency fund can help investors avoid falling into debt traps.

4. Flexibility and Opportunity: Having an emergency fund allows investors to respond to opportunities and unexpected events without disrupting their financial plans. Whether it's seizing a lucrative investment opportunity, making a career change, or handling a sudden expense, an emergency fund provides the flexibility to navigate life's uncertainties with confidence.

Building an emergency fund involves setting aside a portion of income regularly and maintaining it in a highly liquid and easily accessible account, such as a savings account or a money market fund. Financial advisors typically recommend saving three to six months' worth of living expenses in an emergency fund to cover essential costs in the event of a financial emergency.

In conclusion, investment risk management is a critical aspect of financial planning that requires investors to assess risks, implement appropriate risk mitigation strategies, and prioritize building emergency funds. By understanding the various types of risks they face, diversifying their portfolios, and maintaining a reserve of liquid assets, investors can enhance their financial resilience and achieve their long-term financial objectives. A proactive approach to risk management can help investors navigate changing market conditions, protect their investments, and secure their financial well-being in the face of uncertainty.

Chapter 7: Investing for Retirement

Retirement planning is a crucial aspect of financial management that requires careful consideration and strategic decision-making to ensure a comfortable and secure future. In this chapter, we will delve deeply into the various components of retirement planning, including retirement accounts such as 401(k), IRA, and Roth IRA, Social Security benefits, and planning for retirement income. By understanding these key elements, individuals can make informed decisions and take proactive steps to build a solid financial foundation for their retirement years.

Retirement Accounts

One of the primary pillars of retirement planning is the utilization of retirement accounts, which are specifically designed to help individuals save and invest for their retirement. There are several types of retirement accounts available, each with its own set of rules, benefits, and tax implications. In this section, we will explore three popular retirement accounts: 401(k), IRA, and Roth IRA.

1. 401(k)

A 401(k) is a retirement savings plan offered by employers that allows employees to contribute a portion of their pre-tax income towards their retirement savings. One of the key advantages of a 401(k) is that contributions are deducted from your paycheck before taxes are withheld, which can lower your taxable income and potentially reduce your current tax liability. In addition, many employers offer matching contributions, where they will match a certain percentage of the employee's contributions, effectively doubling the amount of money saved for retirement.

For example, let's say you earn $50,000 per year and contribute 5% of your salary to your 401(k). If your employer offers a 50% match, they will contribute an additional 2.5% of your salary, resulting in a total contribution of 7.5% of your salary towards your retirement savings.

It's important to note that there are limits on how much you can contribute to a 401(k) each year, which are set by the IRS. For 2021, the contribution limit is $19,500 for individuals under the age of 50, and $26,000 for those aged 50 and older.

2. IRA (Individual Retirement Account)

An Individual Retirement Account (IRA) is a retirement savings account that individuals can open independently of their employer. There are two main types of IRAs: traditional IRA and Roth IRA. A traditional IRA allows individuals to make tax-deductible contributions, which can reduce their taxable income for the year in which the contribution is made. However, withdrawals in retirement are taxed as ordinary income.

On the other hand, a Roth IRA allows individuals to make after-tax contributions, meaning contributions are not tax-deductible, but qualified withdrawals in retirement are tax-free. This can be advantageous for individuals who expect to be in a higher tax bracket in retirement or who want to minimize their tax liability during retirement.

Like 401(k) accounts, there are annual contribution limits for IRAs, with the limit for 2021 set at $6,000 for individuals under the age of 50, and $7,000 for those aged 50 and older.

3. Roth IRA

A Roth IRA is a retirement account that offers tax-free growth and tax-free withdrawals in retirement, making it an attractive option for individuals who want to maximize their tax savings in retirement. Contributions to a Roth IRA are made with after-tax dollars, meaning you don't get a tax deduction for contributing, but the money grows tax-free and can be withdrawn tax-free in retirement.

One of the key benefits of a Roth IRA is that there are no required minimum distributions (RMDs) during the account holder's lifetime, unlike traditional IRAs and 401(k)s which require withdrawals to begin at a certain age. This flexibility can be advantageous for individuals who do not need to access their retirement savings immediately and want to preserve their assets for future generations.

Social Security Benefits

In addition to personal savings and retirement accounts, Social Security benefits play a crucial role in providing income for retirees. Social Security is a federal program that provides retirement, disability, and survivor benefits to eligible individuals. Workers earn Social Security "credits" based on their earnings and contributions to the program, and these credits determine eligibility for benefits.

Social Security retirement benefits are based on your lifetime earnings, so the more you earn over your working years, the higher your benefit amount will be. The age at which you claim Social Security benefits also affects the amount you receive. You can start collecting Social Security retirement benefits as early as age 62, but your benefit amount will be reduced if you claim before your Full Retirement Age (FRA), which is around 66 to 67, depending on your birth year. On the other hand, you can delay claiming Social Security benefits beyond your FRA, up to age 70, which will increase your benefit amount.

For example, if your FRA is 66 and you claim benefits at age 62, your benefit amount will be reduced by around 25-30%. Conversely, if you wait until age 70 to claim benefits, your benefit amount will increase by around 8% for each year you delay, up to a maximum of 32% for those with an FRA of 66. By strategically planning when to claim Social Security benefits, individuals can maximize their lifetime benefits and secure a more comfortable retirement.

Planning for Retirement Income

CHAPTER 7: INVESTING FOR RETIREMENT

Once you have a clear understanding of retirement accounts and Social Security benefits, the next step is to develop a comprehensive strategy for generating retirement income that will sustain you throughout your retirement years. Planning for retirement income involves assessing your financial needs, sources of income, expenses, and potential risks, and creating a plan to ensure a secure and stress-free retirement.

1. Assessing Financial Needs

The first step in planning for retirement income is to assess your financial needs by estimating how much income you will require during retirement to maintain your desired lifestyle. Start by calculating your expected expenses in retirement, including housing costs, healthcare expenses, leisure activities, and any other expenses you anticipate. Consider factors such as inflation, healthcare costs, and potential long-term care needs that may impact your expenses in retirement.

Next, evaluate your potential sources of retirement income, such as Social Security benefits, pension income, retirement account withdrawals, and investment income. Calculate the total income you expect to receive from these sources and compare it to your estimated expenses to determine if there is a shortfall or surplus. If there is a shortfall, you may need to adjust your retirement savings goals or consider other strategies to generate additional income.

2. Sources of Retirement Income

Retirement income can come from various sources, each with

its own characteristics and considerations. Some of the primary sources of retirement income include:

- Social Security Benefits: Social Security is a key source of retirement income for many Americans. By understanding how Social Security benefits are calculated and the impact of claiming decisions on benefit amounts, individuals can maximize their Social Security income and ensure a stable retirement.

- Pension Income: If you are fortunate enough to have a pension from your employer, this can provide a guaranteed stream of income in retirement. Consider factors such as pension payout options, survivor benefits, and inflation protection when evaluating your pension income.

- Retirement Accounts: 401(k), IRA, and Roth IRA accounts can provide a significant portion of your retirement income through withdrawals and distributions. Develop a withdrawal strategy that balances your income needs with tax considerations and ensures your retirement savings last throughout your retirement years.

- Investment Income: Investments such as stocks, bonds, mutual funds, and real estate can generate income in retirement through dividends, interest, and capital gains. Diversify your investment portfolio to manage risk and maximize returns, and consider factors such as asset allocation, risk tolerance, and investment time horizon when planning for retirement income.

3. Distribution Strategies

CHAPTER 7: INVESTING FOR RETIREMENT

When it comes to generating retirement income from your retirement accounts, it's important to develop a distribution strategy that aligns with your financial goals, tax situation, and risk tolerance. There are several strategies you can use to withdraw funds from your retirement accounts, each with its own implications and considerations:

- Systematic Withdrawals: A common approach to retirement income planning is systematic withdrawals, where you withdraw a fixed amount or percentage of your retirement savings each year to cover your expenses. This can provide a predictable income stream but may not adjust for market fluctuations or changes in your financial needs.

- Required Minimum Distributions (RMDs): Starting at age 72, you are required to begin taking minimum distributions from your traditional IRA and 401(k) accounts each year. The amount of the RMD is based on your age, account balance, and life expectancy. Failure to take RMDs can result in substantial penalties, so it's important to plan for these distributions in advance.

- Bucket Strategy: The bucket strategy involves dividing your retirement savings into different "buckets" based on when you will need the money. For example, you might have a cash bucket for short-term expenses, a bond bucket for medium-term income, and a stock bucket for long-term growth. By strategically allocating your assets across these buckets, you can manage risk, maintain liquidity, and generate income throughout retirement.

- Annuities: Annuities are financial products that provide a guaranteed stream of income for a set period or for life. Fixed annuities offer a fixed income, while variable annuities offer income that varies based on the performance of underlying investments. Consider the fees, surrender charges, and long-term implications of annuities before incorporating them into your retirement income plan.

4. Managing Risks

Lastly, retirement income planning involves managing various risks that can impact your financial security in retirement. Some common risks to consider when planning for retirement income include:

- Longevity Risk: The risk of outliving your retirement savings is a significant concern for many retirees. To mitigate longevity risk, consider strategies such as delaying Social Security benefits, annuitizing a portion of your retirement savings, and maintaining a diversified investment portfolio that can withstand market fluctuations.

- Inflation Risk: Inflation erodes the purchasing power of your retirement income over time, reducing your standard of living in retirement. To combat inflation risk, invest in assets that offer inflation protection, such as Treasury Inflation-Protected Securities (TIPS), and consider adjusting your retirement income for inflation annually to maintain your purchasing power.

- Market Risk: Fluctuations in the financial markets can impact the value of your retirement investments and the income generated from them. To manage market risk, diversify your investment portfolio across different asset classes, rebalance regularly to maintain your target asset allocation, and stay focused on your long-term investment goals rather than short-term market volatility.

- Healthcare Costs: Healthcare expenses can be a significant burden in retirement, especially as you age and require more medical care. Factor in the cost of healthcare when planning for retirement income, explore options for health insurance coverage, and consider long-term care insurance to protect your assets from the high cost of long-term care services.

By incorporating these strategies and considerations into your retirement income plan, you can create a resilient financial strategy that supports your lifestyle goals and provides peace of mind throughout your retirement years.

Conclusion

Retirement planning is a lifelong journey that requires careful consideration, strategic planning, and proactive decision-making to ensure a secure and comfortable retirement. By understanding the key components of retirement planning, including retirement accounts such as 401(k), IRA, and Roth IRA, Social Security benefits, and planning for retirement income, individuals can make informed choices that align with their financial goals and priorities.

Whether you are just starting your career or approaching retirement age, it's never too early or too late to begin planning for your retirement. Take the time to assess your financial needs, explore different sources of retirement income, develop a comprehensive retirement income plan, and proactively manage risks to secure a stable and fulfilling retirement.

Remember that retirement planning is a dynamic process that requires regular review and adjustments as your circumstances change. By staying informed, seeking professional guidance when needed, and staying committed to your long-term financial goals, you can build a solid foundation for a rewarding retirement that reflects your values, aspirations, and legacy. Start today and embark on the journey to a secure and prosperous retirement future.

Chapter 8: Tax Considerations in Investing

In Chapter 8 of our guide, we delve into one of the critical aspects of investing that often gets overlooked—tax considerations. Understanding the tax implications of your investments is crucial for maximizing your returns and optimizing your portfolio. In this chapter, we will explore three key topics: Capital Gains Tax, Dividend Tax, and Tax-Efficient Investing. We will discuss each of these concepts in detail, providing examples and practical insights to help you navigate the complex world of taxation in investing.

1. Capital Gains Tax:

Capital gains tax is a tax levied on the profit realized from the sale of an asset such as stocks, bonds, real estate, or other investments. The tax is calculated based on the difference between the purchase price (cost basis) and the selling price of the asset. Capital gains can be classified into two categories: short-term capital gains and long-term capital gains, each with different tax rates.

Short-term capital gains: Short-term capital gains refer to profits earned from the sale of an asset held for one year or less. In most countries, short-term gains are taxed at higher rates than long-term gains, as they are considered part of the investor's regular income. For example, in the United States, short-term capital gains are taxed at the taxpayer's ordinary income tax rate, which can range from 10% to 37% based on the individual's income level.

Example: Sarah purchased 100 shares of XYZ Company at $50 per share in January and sold them in July for $70 per share. Since Sarah held the shares for less than a year, her capital gain of $20 per share would be subject to short-term capital gains tax based on her ordinary income tax rate.

Long-term capital gains: Long-term capital gains, on the other hand, refer to profits earned from the sale of an asset held for more than one year. In many countries, including the United States, long-term capital gains are subject to preferential tax rates, which are usually lower than ordinary income tax rates. Lower tax rates on long-term investments are aimed at encouraging long-term investment and capital formation.

Example: John purchased 100 shares of ABC Company at $40 per share three years ago and sold them for $60 per share. Since John held the shares for more than a year, his capital gain of $20 per share would be subject to long-term capital gains tax, which is typically lower than the ordinary income tax rate.

Tax-loss harvesting: Investors can offset capital gains by realizing losses on other investments in a strategy known as tax-loss harvesting. By selling investments that have declined in value, investors can use the losses to offset capital gains and reduce their tax liabilities. Tax-loss harvesting can be a useful tool for optimizing tax efficiency in a portfolio.

2. Dividend Tax:

Dividend tax is a tax imposed on the income investors receive from dividend-paying stocks and mutual funds. Dividends are distributions of a company's profits to its shareholders and can be classified into two categories: qualified dividends and non-qualified dividends, each with different tax treatment.

Qualified dividends: Qualified dividends are dividends paid by U.S. corporations or qualified foreign corporations that meet certain criteria set by the Internal Revenue Service (IRS). Qualified dividends are taxed at long-term capital gains tax rates, which are lower than ordinary income tax rates. To qualify for preferential tax treatment, dividends must be held for a minimum period, usually more than 60 days during the 121-day period that begins 60 days before the ex-dividend date.

Example: Emily received $1,000 in qualified dividends from her investments in XYZ Corporation. Since the dividends meet the criteria for qualified status, they would be subject to long-term capital gains tax rates when included in Emily's taxable income.

Non-qualified dividends: Non-qualified dividends include dividends that do not meet the requirements for qualified status, such as dividends from real estate investment trusts (REITs), master limited partnerships (MLPs), and certain foreign corporations. Non-qualified dividends are taxed at the investor's ordinary income tax rate, which can be significantly higher than the rates applied to qualified dividends.

Example: Mark received $1,000 in non-qualified dividends from his investments in a real estate investment trust. Since the dividends do not meet the criteria for qualified status, they would be subject to Mark's ordinary income tax rate when included in his taxable income.

Double taxation of dividends: Dividends are subject to double taxation in some cases, meaning that the profits distributed by a company are taxed at both the corporate level and the individual level. This can result in a higher overall tax burden for investors receiving dividends, especially in countries where corporate tax rates are high.

3. Tax-Efficient Investing:

Tax-efficient investing is a strategy aimed at minimizing the tax impact of investment returns by optimizing the structure and location of investments within a portfolio. By strategically managing investments in different types of accounts, such as taxable accounts, tax-deferred accounts (e.g., traditional IRAs, 401(k)s), and tax-exempt accounts (e.g., Roth IRAs), investors can reduce their tax liabilities and enhance their after-tax returns.

Asset location: Asset location refers to the placement of specific types of investments in different types of accounts to maximize tax efficiency. Tax-efficient asset location involves placing tax-inefficient investments, such as bonds or real estate investment trusts (REITs), in tax-deferred or tax-exempt accounts, where their tax implications are minimized. Meanwhile, tax-efficient investments, such as index funds or growth stocks with lower dividend yields, can be held in taxable accounts to take advantage of preferential tax treatment on capital gains.

Example: Lisa holds a diversified portfolio consisting of stocks and bonds in both taxable and tax-deferred accounts. To optimize tax efficiency, Lisa places her bond investments, which generate interest income taxed at ordinary income rates, in her tax-deferred IRA account. On the other hand, she holds her stock investments, which have the potential for capital appreciation and lower tax implications, in her taxable brokerage account.

Tax-loss harvesting: As mentioned earlier, tax-loss harvesting involves selling investments at a loss to offset capital gains and reduce tax liabilities. By strategically realizing losses on investments in taxable accounts, investors can generate tax deductions that can be used to offset capital gains or up to $3,000 of ordinary income per year. Additionally, harvested losses can be carried forward to future years to offset gains or income.

Roth conversion: A Roth conversion involves transferring funds from a traditional IRA or 401(k) to a Roth IRA, where investments can grow tax-free and qualified withdrawals are not subject to taxation. While Roth conversions result in immediate tax liabilities on the converted amount, they can be advantageous in the long run, especially if investors expect to be in a higher tax bracket in retirement or anticipate tax law changes that could result in higher tax rates.

Tax-efficient investments: Investing in tax-efficient vehicles, such as index funds, exchange-traded funds (ETFs), and municipal bonds, can help reduce tax liabilities and enhance after-tax returns. Index funds and ETFs typically have lower turnover rates compared to actively managed mutual funds, resulting in fewer capital gains distributions and lower tax consequences for investors. Municipal bonds, which are issued by state and local governments and exempt from federal income tax, can provide tax-free income to investors in higher tax brackets.

Diversification: Diversification is a key principle of investing that also applies to tax efficiency. By diversifying investments across different asset classes, sectors, and geographies, investors can spread risk and potentially reduce the impact of taxes on their overall portfolio. Diversification can help mitigate the tax consequences of concentrated holdings that may be subject to higher tax rates or risks.

In conclusion, understanding the tax implications of investing is crucial for optimizing portfolio performance and achieving long-term financial goals. By considering factors such as capital gains tax, dividend tax, and tax-efficient investing strategies, investors can minimize tax liabilities, preserve more of their investment returns, and enhance the after-tax value of their portfolios. While navigating the complexities of taxation in investing may seem daunting, seeking guidance from financial professionals and staying informed about tax laws and regulations can empower investors to make informed decisions and build tax-efficient investment strategies.

Chapter 9: Evaluating Investment Performance

Investing is a critical aspect of personal finance management and wealth building. Once you have set up your investment portfolio, it is essential to monitor and evaluate its performance regularly. Monitoring helps you stay informed about how your investments are doing and whether they align with your financial goals. Additionally, rebalancing your portfolio ensures that your asset allocation remains in line with your risk tolerance and objectives. In this chapter, we will delve into the details of evaluating investment performance, monitoring investments, rebalancing a portfolio, and key investment performance metrics.

Monitoring Your Investments

Monitoring your investments is crucial to ensure that they are on track to help you achieve your financial objectives. Regularly reviewing the performance of your investments allows you to identify areas that need attention and make informed decisions to optimize your portfolio. Here are some key aspects to consider when monitoring your investments:

1. Reviewing Portfolio Allocations: It is essential to review the allocation of your investments across various asset classes, such as stocks, bonds, and alternative investments. Monitoring your asset allocation helps you maintain a diversified portfolio and manage risk effectively.

2. Assessing Individual Investments: Evaluate the performance of individual investments within your portfolio. Understand how each investment contributes to your overall returns and whether they are meeting your expectations.

3. Analyzing Risk and Return: Monitor the risk and return profile of your investments. Assess whether the level of risk you are taking aligns with your risk tolerance and evaluate the returns generated relative to the risk incurred.

4. Tracking Costs: Keep track of the costs associated with your investments, such as management fees, transaction costs, and taxes. High costs can erode your returns over time, so it is essential to assess the impact of fees on your investment performance.

5. Monitoring Market Trends: Stay informed about market trends, economic developments, and geopolitical events that can impact your investments. Understanding the broader market environment can help you make informed decisions about your portfolio.

6. Setting Realistic Goals: Regularly review your investment goals and objectives to ensure that they are still relevant and achievable. Adjust your goals as needed based on changes in

your financial situation or market conditions.

Rebalancing Your Portfolio

Portfolio rebalancing involves adjusting the allocation of assets in your portfolio to maintain a desired risk-return profile. Over time, changes in asset values can cause your portfolio to deviate from your target asset allocation. Rebalancing ensures that you realign your portfolio to match your original investment strategy. Here are some key points to consider when rebalancing your portfolio:

1. Asset Allocation Targets: Determine your target asset allocation based on your financial goals, risk tolerance, and investment horizon. Your asset allocation should reflect a balance between risk and return that aligns with your investment objectives.

2. Monitoring Drift: Regularly monitor the actual allocation of assets in your portfolio to identify any drift from your target allocation. Asset classes that have outperformed may become overweight, while underperforming assets may become underweight.

3. Rebalancing Strategies: There are several strategies you can use to rebalance your portfolio, including:
   - Time-Based Rebalancing: Rebalance your portfolio at regular intervals (e.g., annually) to maintain your target asset allocation.
   - Threshold Rebalancing: Rebalance your portfolio when the allocation of a specific asset class deviates beyond a certain

threshold (e.g., +/- 5%).

- Cash Flows Rebalancing: Use cash inflows or outflows from your investment accounts to rebalance your portfolio by investing in underweight or overweight asset classes.

- Tactical Rebalancing: Take advantage of market conditions or economic trends to adjust your asset allocation strategically.

4. Tax Considerations: Be mindful of tax implications when rebalancing your portfolio. Selling appreciated assets may trigger capital gains taxes, so consider tax-efficient strategies to rebalance your portfolio.

5. Implementation: Once you have decided to rebalance your portfolio, execute the necessary trades to realign your asset allocation. Monitor the impact of the rebalancing on your portfolio's risk and return characteristics.

Investment Performance Metrics

Evaluating investment performance requires using various metrics to assess how well your investments are performing relative to your expectations and benchmarks. These performance metrics provide insights into the returns, risk, and efficiency of your portfolio. Here are some key investment performance metrics to consider:

1. Return on Investment (ROI): ROI measures the gain or loss generated on an investment relative to its cost. It is calculated as:

\[ROI = \frac{(Current Value of Investment - Cost of Investment)}{Cost of Investment} \times 100%\]

For example, if you bought a stock for $1,000 and its current value is $1,200, your ROI would be \[($1,200 - $1,000)/$1,000 \times 100% = 20%\].

2. Annualized Return: Annualized return calculates the average rate of return per year over a specific period. It is useful for comparing the performance of investments with different holding periods. The formula for annualized return is:

\[Annualized Return = \left(1 + \frac{Total Return}{Initial Investment}\right) ^ {\frac{1}{\text{Number of Years}}} - 1\]

3. Standard Deviation: Standard deviation measures the volatility or risk of an investment. A higher standard deviation indicates greater price variability, while a lower standard deviation suggests more stable returns. It is a measure of the dispersion of returns around the average return.

4. Sharpe Ratio: The Sharpe ratio measures the risk-adjusted return of an investment and helps investors evaluate the return generated per unit of risk taken. A higher Sharpe ratio indicates better risk-adjusted performance. The formula for Sharpe ratio is:

\[Sharpe Ratio = \frac{(Portfolio Return - Risk-Free Rate)}{Portfolio Standard Deviation}\]

5. Treynor Ratio: The Treynor ratio measures the risk-adjusted return of a portfolio relative to its systematic risk (beta). It

evaluates the return generated per unit of systematic risk. The formula for Treynor ratio is:

$$Treynor\ Ratio = \frac{(Portfolio\ Return - Risk\text{-}Free\ Rate)}{Portfolio\ Beta}$$

6. Alpha: Alpha measures the excess return of an investment compared to its expected return based on its risk level. A positive alpha indicates outperformance relative to the risk taken, while a negative alpha suggests underperformance.

7. Information Ratio: The Information ratio measures the excess return of a portfolio relative to its benchmark index per unit of active risk taken. It evaluates the ability of a portfolio manager to generate excess returns beyond the benchmark.

8. Tracking Error: Tracking error quantifies the variability in returns between a portfolio and its benchmark index. A higher tracking error indicates greater deviation from the benchmark, while a lower tracking error suggests closer tracking.

By utilizing these investment performance metrics, investors can gain a comprehensive understanding of how their investments are performing, analyze the risk-adjusted returns, and make informed decisions to optimize their portfolio.

In conclusion, evaluating investment performance is a critical aspect of successful investing. Monitoring your investments, rebalancing your portfolio, and analyzing key performance metrics are essential tasks to ensure that your investment strategy remains aligned with your financial goals. By actively managing your investments and regularly assessing their performance, you can make informed decisions to enhance your portfolio's returns and manage risk effectively. Remember that investment performance evaluation is an ongoing process that requires diligence, discipline, and a thorough understanding of your investment objectives.

Chapter 10: Investing in the Digital Age

Investing in the digital age has been reshaped and reinvented by technological advancements that have revolutionized the way people manage their finances. In this chapter, we will delve into three key aspects of investing in the digital age: Robo-Advisors, Cryptocurrency and Blockchain Technology, and Online Trading Platforms. These tools and technologies have democratized investing, making it more accessible, efficient, and transparent for a wider range of individuals. We will explore each of these topics in detail, discussing their features, benefits, risks, and providing relevant examples to illustrate their impact on the investing landscape.

Robo-Advisors:

Robo-advisors are automated, algorithm-based investment platforms that provide financial advice and portfolio management with minimal human intervention. These digital tools use algorithms to analyze an investor's financial situation, goals, risk tolerance, and time horizon to create a diversified investment portfolio tailored to their needs. Robo-advisors have gained popularity in recent years due to their low fees, accessibility, and convenience.

Features of Robo-Advisors:

1. Automated Portfolio Management: Robo-advisors use algorithms to automatically manage and rebalance investment portfolios based on specified parameters and market conditions.

2. Goal-Based Investing: Investors can set specific financial goals, such as retirement savings or buying a house, and robo-advisors will recommend an investment strategy to help achieve those goals.

3. Diversification: Robo-advisors typically create diversified portfolios using a mix of asset classes, reducing risk and maximizing returns.

4. Low Fees: Robo-advisors often have lower fees compared to traditional financial advisors, making investing more cost-effective for individual investors.

5. Accessibility: Robo-advisors offer easy sign-up processes and user-friendly interfaces, allowing individuals with different levels of investment knowledge to use their services.

Benefits of Robo-Advisors:

1. Cost-Effective Investing: Robo-advisors offer low fees, making them an affordable option for investors who want to save on management costs.

2. Accessibility: Robo-advisors cater to a wide range of investors, including beginners and those with limited investment experience.

3. Automated Rebalancing: Robo-advisors automatically rebalance portfolios to maintain desired asset allocations, saving investors time and effort.

4. Personalized Advice: Robo-advisors use algorithms to provide tailored investment recommendations based on individual financial goals and risk profiles.

5. Transparency: Robo-advisors provide clear and accessible information about investment choices, fees, and performance to help investors make informed decisions.

Risks of Robo-Advisors:

1. Lack of Human Interaction: Some investors may prefer personalized advice from a human financial advisor, which robo-advisors may not provide.

2. Limited Customization: Robo-advisors may offer limited customization options compared to traditional financial advisors who can tailor investment strategies more precisely.

3. Algorithm Risk: The algorithms used by robo-advisors may not always accurately predict market movements or adjust portfolios effectively in volatile market conditions.

4. Security Concerns: Investors may have concerns about the security of their personal and financial information when using online robo-advisor platforms.

Examples:

1. Betterment: Betterment is a popular robo-advisor platform that offers automated investment management services with personalized advice based on individual financial goals and risk tolerance.

2. Wealthfront: Wealthfront is another well-known robo-advisor that provides low-cost investment management services using advanced algorithms to optimize portfolios and tax efficiency.

3. Vanguard Personal Advisor Services: Vanguard offers a hybrid model that combines robo-advisor technology with access to human financial advisors for personalized advice and guidance.

Overall, robo-advisors have transformed the investment landscape by providing efficient, low-cost investment solutions that cater to a wide range of investors. Their automated portfolio management, goal-based investing approach, and cost-effectiveness make them an attractive option for individuals looking to grow their wealth and achieve their financial goals.

Cryptocurrency and Blockchain Technology:

Cryptocurrency and blockchain technology have disrupted traditional financial systems by introducing decentralized, digital currencies that offer secure and transparent transactions. Cryptocurrencies like Bitcoin, Ethereum, and Ripple have gained popularity as alternative investment assets, while blockchain technology has been hailed for its potential to revolutionize various industries beyond finance. In this section, we will explore the concepts of cryptocurrency and blockchain technology, their features, benefits, risks, and their impact on the investment landscape.

Cryptocurrency:

Cryptocurrency is a digital or virtual form of currency that uses cryptography for security and operates independently of a central authority like a government or financial institution. Cryptocurrencies are built on blockchain technology, a decentralized and transparent ledger that records all transactions securely. Investors can buy, sell, and trade cryptocurrencies on various online exchanges, making them a popular investment option for those seeking diversification in their portfolios.

Features of Cryptocurrency:
1. Decentralization: Cryptocurrencies operate on decentral-

ized networks, eliminating the need for central authorities and enabling peer-to-peer transactions.

2. Security: Cryptocurrencies use cryptographic encryption to secure transactions and prevent fraud, making them more secure than traditional financial systems.

3. Transparency: Blockchain technology ensures that all transactions are recorded on a public ledger that is immutable and transparent, enhancing trust and accountability.

4. Limited Supply: Many cryptocurrencies have a finite supply, such as Bitcoin, which creates scarcity and can impact their value over time.

5. Borderless Transactions: Cryptocurrencies enable cross-border transactions without the need for currency conversions or intermediaries, reducing costs and processing times.

Benefits of Cryptocurrency:

1. Diversification: Cryptocurrencies offer investors an alternative asset class that can help diversify their investment portfolios and hedge against traditional market risks.

2. Potential High Returns: Some cryptocurrencies have experienced significant price appreciation over time, providing investors with the potential for high returns on their investments.

3. Accessible Investment Options: Cryptocurrencies are accessible to individual investors worldwide, allowing anyone with an internet connection to participate in the market.

4. Financial Inclusion: Cryptocurrencies can provide financial services to unbanked populations who may not have access to traditional banking systems, promoting financial inclusion.

5. Innovation: Cryptocurrencies and blockchain technology have paved the way for innovation in finance, technology, and

other industries, driving new business models and opportunities.

Risks of Cryptocurrency:

1. Price Volatility: Cryptocurrencies are known for their price volatility, with sharp fluctuations that can result in significant gains or losses for investors.

2. Regulatory Uncertainty: The regulatory landscape for cryptocurrencies is still evolving, with differing approaches across countries and regions that can impact market stability.

3. Security Risks: Cryptocurrency exchanges and wallets are vulnerable to hacks and cyberattacks, leading to the loss of funds and personal information for investors.

4. Lack of Consumer Protection: Unlike traditional financial systems, cryptocurrencies offer limited consumer protection mechanisms, exposing investors to higher levels of risk.

5. Market Manipulation: The cryptocurrency market is susceptible to manipulation and fraud due to its decentralized nature, lack of oversight, and low liquidity in some cases.

Examples:

1. Bitcoin: Bitcoin is the first and most well-known cryptocurrency, created by an anonymous individual or group known as Satoshi Nakamoto. It operates on a decentralized network and has a limited supply of 21 million coins.

2. Ethereum: Ethereum is a blockchain platform that enables developers to build decentralized applications (DApps) and smart contracts. Its native cryptocurrency is called Ether (ETH).

3. Ripple: Ripple is a digital payment protocol that enables fast and low-cost cross-border transactions. Its native cryptocurrency is called XRP and is used to facilitate transfers on the

Ripple network.

Despite the risks associated with cryptocurrencies, their growing popularity and potential for innovation have made them a compelling investment option for individuals looking to diversify their portfolios and capitalize on the benefits of blockchain technology. As the cryptocurrency market continues to evolve, investors should carefully consider the risks and rewards of investing in this dynamic asset class.

Blockchain Technology:
Blockchain technology serves as the underlying framework for cryptocurrencies, providing a secure and transparent way to record transactions on a decentralized ledger. Beyond its applications in digital currencies, blockchain technology has the potential to revolutionize various industries, including finance, healthcare, supply chain management, and more. By leveraging its features of decentralization, transparency, security, and immutability, blockchain technology offers opportunities for increased efficiency, trust, and innovation in traditional business processes.

Features of Blockchain Technology:
1. Decentralization: Blockchain technology operates on a network of distributed nodes that work together to validate transactions and maintain a secure ledger without the need for a central authority.
2. Transparency: All transactions on a blockchain are recorded on a public ledger that is visible to all participants, enhancing trust and accountability within the network.
3. Security: Blockchain uses cryptographic encryption and

consensus mechanisms to secure transactions and prevent unauthorized tampering or fraud.

4. Immutability: Once a transaction is recorded on a blockchain, it cannot be altered or deleted, ensuring the integrity and reliability of the data.

5. Smart Contracts: Smart contracts are self-executing agreements recorded on a blockchain that automatically enforce the terms of a contract when predefined conditions are met, reducing the need for intermediaries and increasing automation.

Benefits of Blockchain Technology:

1. Enhanced Security: Blockchain technology provides a secure and transparent way to record transactions, reducing the risk of fraud, manipulation, and data breaches.

2. Increased Efficiency: By automating processes and eliminating intermediaries, blockchain technology can streamline business operations, reduce costs, and improve the speed of transactions.

3. Greater Transparency: The transparency of blockchain ledgers enhances trust among participants by providing a clear record of transactions and ensuring data integrity.

4. Cost Savings: Blockchain technology can reduce costs associated with third-party intermediaries, paperwork, and manual processes, leading to overall cost savings for businesses.

5. Innovation Opportunities: Blockchain technology enables new business models, digital assets, and decentralized applications that can drive innovation across various industries and create new opportunities for growth.

Risks of Blockchain Technology:

1. Scalability Challenges: Blockchain networks face scalability

limitations in terms of transaction throughput, processing speed, and energy consumption, which can hinder widespread adoption.

2. Regulatory Uncertainty: The regulatory landscape for blockchain technology is still evolving, with differing approaches across jurisdictions that can impact its growth and development.

3. Privacy Concerns: While blockchain offers transparency and security, privacy concerns arise regarding the exposure of personal or sensitive data on a public ledger.

4. Interoperability Issues: Different blockchain platforms may have interoperability challenges, making it difficult to transfer assets and data seamlessly between networks.

5. Energy Consumption: Some blockchain networks, like Bitcoin, require substantial energy consumption for mining and processing transactions, leading to environmental concerns.

Examples:

1. Hyperledger: Hyperledger is an open-source blockchain platform developed by the Linux Foundation that supports enterprise blockchain applications and smart contracts.

2. ConsenSys: ConsenSys is a blockchain technology company that builds decentralized applications and tools on the Ethereum ecosystem, focusing on innovation and adoption of blockchain solutions.

3. IBM Blockchain: IBM offers a blockchain platform for businesses to build and deploy blockchain applications across industries, providing solutions for supply chain management, fintech, and more.

In conclusion, blockchain technology has the potential to transform industries by increasing security, transparency, and efficiency in business processes. As organizations explore new use cases and adopt blockchain solutions, investors should monitor developments in this space to identify opportunities for investment and innovation.

Online Trading Platforms:

Online trading platforms have revolutionized the way individuals buy and sell financial securities, providing a convenient and accessible way to invest in stocks, bonds, options, and other assets. These digital platforms offer real-time trading capabilities, research tools, educational resources, and personalized investment insights to help investors make informed decisions and manage their portfolios efficiently. In this section, we will explore the features, benefits, risks, and examples of online trading platforms in the digital age.

Features of Online Trading Platforms:

1. Real-Time Trading: Online trading platforms enable investors to buy and sell financial securities in real-time, providing immediate execution of trades at current market prices.

2. Research Tools: Online trading platforms offer a variety of research tools, including stock screeners, charting software, market news, and analyst reports, to help investors analyze potential investments.

3. Educational Resources: Many online trading platforms provide educational resources such as webinars, tutorials, and articles to help investors improve their knowledge of investing and trading strategies.

4. Portfolio Management: Online trading platforms offer portfolio tracking tools that allow investors to monitor their

investments, track performance, and adjust asset allocations as needed.

5. Mobile Accessibility: Most online trading platforms have mobile applications that enable investors to trade on the go, access market information, and receive notifications about their portfolios.

Benefits of Online Trading Platforms:

1. Convenience: Online trading platforms offer 24/7 access to financial markets, allowing investors to trade from anywhere with an internet connection and a computer or mobile device.

2. Cost-Effective Trading: Online trading platforms typically have lower fees and commissions compared to traditional brokerage services, making investing more affordable for individual investors.

3. Real-Time Information: Online trading platforms provide real-time market data, news updates, and research tools to help investors make informed decisions and react quickly to market developments.

4. Control and Flexibility: Investors have greater control over their investment decisions and can customize their trading strategies, asset allocations, and risk levels using online trading platforms.

5. Global Market Access: Online trading platforms offer access to a wide range of financial markets, including stocks, bonds, commodities, and currencies, allowing investors to diversify their portfolios globally.

Risks of Online Trading Platforms:

1. Market Volatility: Online trading platforms expose investors to market volatility, with prices of financial securities

fluctuating rapidly based on supply and demand factors.

2. Security Risks: Online trading platforms may be vulnerable to cyberattacks, data breaches, or technical glitches that can compromise the security of investor accounts and assets.

3. Lack of Personalized Advice: While online trading platforms offer research tools and educational resources, they may not provide personalized investment advice or guidance that some investors require.

4. Overtrading: The ease of trading on online platforms can lead to overtrading behavior, where investors make frequent transactions based on emotions or short-term market trends rather than a strategic investment plan.

5. Regulatory Compliance: Online trading platforms must adhere to regulatory requirements, ensure investor protection, and maintain transparency in their operations, which can pose challenges in some jurisdictions.

Examples:

1. ETRADE: ETRADE is an online trading platform that offers a wide range of investment products, research tools, and educational resources for self-directed investors.

2. Robinhood: Robinhood is a commission-free trading platform that has gained popularity for its user-friendly interface, mobile accessibility, and fractional share trading capabilities.

3. TD Ameritrade: TD Ameritrade is an online brokerage platform that provides an array of investment options, trading tools, and educational materials for investors of all levels.

As online trading platforms continue to evolve and innovate, investors can take advantage of their convenience, cost-effectiveness, and access to global markets to build and manage their investment portfolios effectively. By leveraging the features and benefits of these platforms while being aware of the associated risks, investors can navigate the digital landscape of investing in a dynamic and efficient manner.

Conclusion:

Investing in the digital age has been transformed by technological advancements that have democratized access to financial markets, expanded investment options, and empowered individuals to take control of their financial futures. Robo-advisors, cryptocurrency and blockchain technology, and online trading platforms are just a few examples of the innovative tools and technologies that have reshaped the investing landscape, offering new opportunities and challenges for investors worldwide.

Robo-advisors have simplified investment management with automated portfolio allocation, goal-based investing, and low-cost fees, making it easier for individuals to invest and grow their wealth. Cryptocurrency and blockchain technology have introduced digital currencies and decentralized ledgers that provide alternative investment options and innovative solutions for various industries. Online trading platforms have revolutionized the way investors buy and sell financial assets, offering real-time trading capabilities, research tools, and mobile accessibility to enhance the investing experience.

As investors navigate the digital age of investing, it is essential to understand the features, benefits, risks, and examples of these digital tools and technologies to make informed decisions and optimize their investment strategies. By leveraging the opportunities presented by robo-advisors, cryptocurrency and blockchain technology, and online trading platforms, investors can capitalize on the benefits of the digital age to achieve their financial goals and build long-term wealth in a rapidly evolving and dynamic investment landscape.

www.ingramcontent.com/pod-product-compliance
Lightning Source LLC
Chambersburg PA
CBHW070355230526
45471CB00006B/2588